ABOUT THE AUTHOR

Born in California USA, Steve began performing at the age of 5 and since has toured, studied, composed, taught and loved music. As a teenager, he began extensive studies on the drums, trombone, guitar, string-bass, vocal training, and song writing. He graduated with honors from Musicians Institute (PIT) in Hollywood California. He continues to compose music regularly. He has toured the United States, Japan, Greenland, Australia and Greece. Early on, he began collecting notes and information for his hobby of spinning drumsticks which evolved into his book, "Drumstick Spinology™".

DISCLAIMER

This book is designed and published to provide information and entertainment in regards to the subject matter covered. It is sold with the understanding that the publisher and author shall have neither liability nor responsibility to any person or entity, in any form, directly or indirectly, in regards to the ideas within.

Every effort has been made to make this book as complete and accurate as possible. However, there may be mistakes typographical and/or in content.

As you spin, practice, and study Drumstick Spinology™, notify the publisher and author of any errors, ideas and suggestions.

TABLE OF CONTENTS

IN WRITING OUT THESE DRUMSTICK SPINS, I found it necessary to invent a system of descriptions using letters, numbers, words, directions, pictures, and diagrams to help express exactly what the various maneuvers called for. The technical information of my system is explained in the beginning of the book (Part I), preparing you to fully understand the actual spins (Part II). I have written, rewritten, and re-rewritten them all several times in an attempt to present this material clearly so that you will be able to understand it easily.

I SUGGEST THAT YOU APPROACH each spin as would a Kung-Fu Master… slowly, patiently, methodically, until the overall picture is seen. Only then can repetition become possible, and the more repetition, the more speed and capability is gained.

I hope my efforts will serve you well.
Steve Stockmal

Spinning drumsticks and playing drums are two different worlds bound by only one thing…the sticks!

The ultimate goal of this book is to teach the student of Spinology how to spin drumsticks, and how to incorporate this knowledge into his/her playing.

To spin or not to spin… that is the question.

ONCE WHILE PLAYING DRUMS in a touring band I was involved in a small accident and cut my left hand. For two or three weeks I was forced to play the entire show utilizing my other three limbs, allowing the injured hand to recover. From that experience I was freed from playing "glued" to the drum set and found myself more willing to take chances with my stick spinning, singing, choreography, etc. because I knew I could always cover the sound with my available hands or feet.

SPINNING THE STICKS enhances what people see in a performance by creating an added dimension, the visual aspect of playing music. The best thing for me to see is a great drummer who occasionally throws in a killer stick-spin, enhancing climactic moments, and filling in the "empty" spaces, thus adding to the show.

BY CONSTANTLY WORKING with the drumsticks, you'll see that your playing actually improves and benefits in several ways. While familiarizing your hands and mind with the size, weight, and feel of the stick, you'll be relaxing and developing the muscles of the fingers and wrists. When I'm touring, and all of my equipment is packed away in a truck, I can still work on my drumming by training with the sticks.

SPINOLOGY IS ALSO a great "sport" to practice because is doesn't make any noise. So, as long as you don't drop the sticks, you can spin for hours in silence. Imagine that…a quiet drummer!

TO MASTER ANYTHING in life takes dedication, persistence, time and inspiration. As I endorse throughout this book–don't neglect your drumming time. Instead, find times to practice spinning when you couldn't play anyway, like late at night, on your way to the next gig, watching TV, etc. Be consistent and stay true to your drumming, because that's where it all comes from.

TO REITERATE, this book gives you the basic tools to develop spinning drumsticks, create your own spins, and help you to expand your style by adding to your performance as a drummer and musician. Not every spin will suit you, or necessarily be practical to your playing, tastes, or abilities. So try them all, find the ones that you like best, and can perform well, and go for it!!! I hope that some of my ideas and suggestions will help to spark your own creativity.

So good luck, may you spin with zeal…and find your place in the world of Drumstick Spinology™, drumming, music, and life.

PART ONE | Preparatory Material

Pertinent Information These are the things you must know in order to understand and use this book to its fullest potential.

Diagram of the Hand This chart shows you my system of identifying the various parts of the hand.

Diagram of the Stick This shows you my system of identifying the different parts of the stick.

Grips Here you'll find all of the ways you will need to hold the sticks.

Directions Now you are shown the different directions in which the stick, your hand, arm, and fingers can move.

Observations This section is a synopsis of technique, some possible traps to watch out for and other miscellaneous information and ideas.

Warming Up Here are some ideas on stretching and pre-conditioning to help you warm up before you start playing or spinning.

PART TWO | Spinning

Chapter 1 **The Basic Spins** Chapter 1 describes the basic spins that will serve as your "vocabulary" for the following pages.

Chapter 2 **Variations** Chapter 2 teaches you more ideas based on the first chapter. You'll learn new ways and directions to toss, spin, catch, and flip the sticks, and many more variations of the Basic Spins from Chapter 1.

Chapter 3 **Application** Chapter 3 introduces you to some practical applications at the drum set so that you'll be able to use your newly acquired knowledge while playing, or during "rests" in the music. At the end of this chapter you will find a page of drum set rhythms that can be played with one hand, while spinning with the other.

Chapter 4 **Combinations** Chapter 4 contains some combinations of spins to form longer routines. Using these and experimenting, you can begin to develop your own style, ideas, and combinations.

Chapter 5 **Humor** Chapter 5 is a compilation of ideas for your entertainment, amusement and imagination, to further inspire your creativity with the drumsticks.

PART ONE

PREPARATORY
MATERIAL

PERTINENT INFORMATION

1   Any word, letter, direction, etc. that is written in CAPITAL LETTERS means that it has a specific meaning as defined in the first part of the book.

2   All spins are explained for the right hand (R) unless otherwise noted. I must however stress the importance of developing both hands equally; so learn with the strong hand, then teach the weaker one to build strength and dexterity.

3   The hand is held in the "hand shaking" position (palm facing left) unless otherwise noted.

4   Unless otherwise noted, the stick is always held in READY POSITION (See GRIPS).

5   When spinning (FORWARD, REVERSE, etc.) the stick spins around Y of the finger (see Diagram of the Hand) unless otherwise noted.

6   When you read "… fingers 1,2,3, & 4…" or "A-B-C" etc. it means that the stick spins specifically in that order past those fingers or slots.

7   When you get to Chapter Two #16, I introduce the concept of WALKING. This means that the hand "walks" (moves) up and down the stick. Practice WALKING to learn how to find the balance point of any spin.

8   FLIP refers to a quick, jerky movement that acts as the catalyst for the momentum of a single action move.

9   SPIN refers to any continuous movement of the stick(s).

HAND DIAGRAM

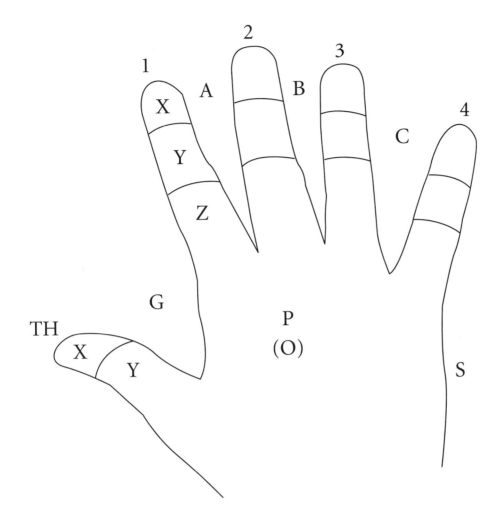

Definition of Symbols

1-2-3-4	The four fingers; INDEX, MIDDLE, RING, and PINKY respectively.
A-B-C-G	The SLOTS between the fingers.
TH	The THUMB.
X-Y-Z	These are the "pads" between the knuckles.
P	Refers to PALM of the hand, or any part of that side of the hand.
O	Refers to the "opposite" side of the hand; the back of the hand.
S	Denotes the "side" of the hand, opposite the thumb.
R	The right hand.
L	The left hand.

STICK DIAGRAM

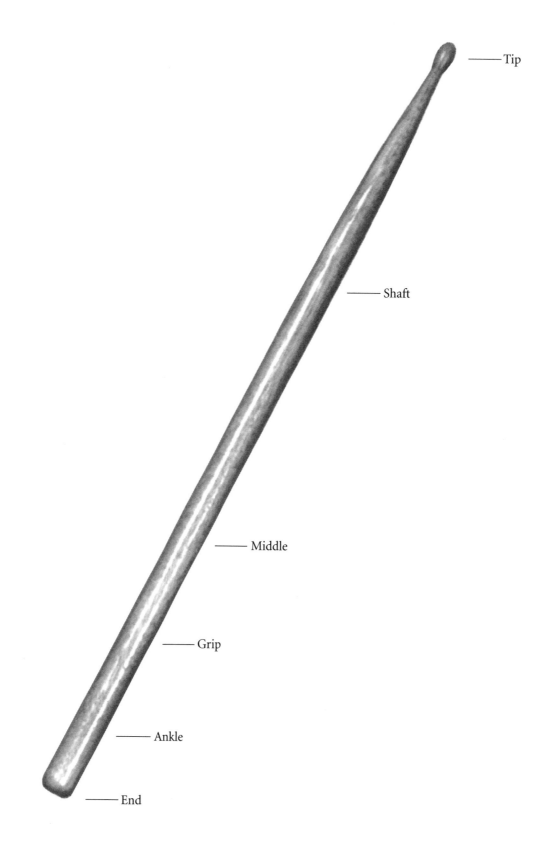

Tip

Shaft

Middle

Grip

Ankle

End

GRIPS

MATCH GRIP
Both sticks are held the same at the GRIP part of the stick by using the thumb and 1st finger as the fulcrum, and fingers 2, 3, & 4 lightly touching the stick.

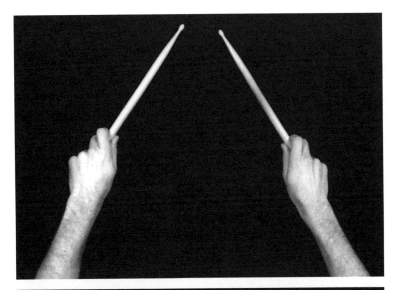

TRADITIONAL GRIP
The right hand is held the same as MATCH GRIP but the left hand holds the stick so that it goes through TH/Y and B/Y with the PALM facing UP.

READY POSITION
The stick is held in MATCH GRIP style, but this time at the MIDDLE of the stick. **Note** For spinning, the stick is usually held at or toward the MIDDLE of the stick, unless otherwise noted.

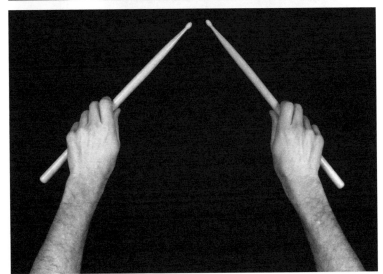

GRIPS

FAKE GRIP
Start from the READY
POSITION, then slide the
1st finger over so that the
stick is in A/Y.
Note You can still play from
this position.

DOUBLE TRADITIONAL
Both sticks are held in
TRADITIONAL GRIP, like the
left hand in #2 above.

BACKWARDS MATCH
Hold the sticks backwards
in MATCH GRIP style by
grabbing the SHAFT.

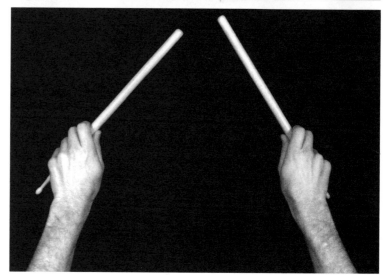

GRIPS

FAKE TRADITIONAL
Same as TRADITIONAL GRIP
but held in A/Y instead of B/Y.

HI HAT PLAYING POSITION
Start with your right hand on the hi hat, and your left hand on the snare drum.

REVERSE HI HAT PLAYING POSITION
Same as above, but with the left hand on the hi hat and the right hand on the snare drum.

RIDE CYMBAL PLAYING POSITION
Start with the right hand on the ride cymbal, and the left hand on the snare drum.

SNARE DRUM PLAYING POSITION
Playing with both hands on the snare drum.

DIRECTIONS

1   **Clockwise** The direction in which clock hands move, when the clock is on the wall (vertical plane) or lying on the ground (horizontal plane).

2   **Counterclockwise** Exactly opposite of CLOCKWISE (#1).

4   **Forward** Refers to the direction that a wheel would spin if it were going away from you.

5   **Reverse** Opposite of #3, this time the wheel is coming toward you.

6   **Figure 8** Refers to the stick spinning a pattern that goes in and out (back and forth) of both sides of your hand.

7   **In** The stick, your arm, or your hand will go toward the center line of your body (i.e. the right hand will move left, or the left hand will go to the right).

8   **Out** Opposite of #7, this time the stick, etc. will go away from your center line.

9   **Up** The stick, arm or hand will move or point toward the sky.

10   **Down** The stick, etc. will move or point toward the ground.

11   **Over** The stick will spin or roll across the top (0) of the hand or fingers.

12   **Under** Opposite of #11, this time the stick spins under the bottom (P) of the hand or fingers.

13   **Front** Facing the audience (i.e. in front of you).

14   **Back** Facing you. For example, "…PALM back…" means that you can see your PALM.

15   **a. Sideways** Any 45° angle.
    b. Reverse sideways goes on a 45° line backwards.

OBSERVATIONS

1 Just as practice and repetition are important, so is improvisation. I suggest practicing these spins many times with strict disciplinary style to master them technically; then try letting the sticks flow through your fingers smoothly and effortlessly, and let the powers of improvisation take you to new places.

2 When you're first starting out, you can use your free hand to help walk the stick around certain difficult patterns, until you develop the muscles and flexibility to manipulate the stick well.

3 Don't forget that your main job is playing the drums, so don't sacrifice the sound for a spin, especially snare hits. Use your spins in convenient, "in-between" moments (see Chapter 3, #22) so that you never lose the quality of the sound, or the flow of the song.

4 If you want, you could add color, fluorescent paint, streamers, tinsel, etc. to add to the visual effect.

5 When your're first learning these spins, you might try practicing while sitting on carpet or grass so that if you drop the sticks they won't roll away, chip or make noise.

6 It would seem that this book is theoretically impossible to finish. The more that I wrote, the more new spins that I invented, and the more I invented the more I would write. I finally decided to publish this book, as there is enough information here to keep the interested student occupied.

7 It is important to consider what to do if you drop a stick while performing so that the song doesn't suffer. There are several places to keep extra sticks. For example, on the bass drum, or in the slot between the bass drum and the tension lug, or in a stick bag hanging from the floor tom, or in your back pocket, or sheathed in your belt. You can invent creative, easy-to-reach places of your own. Just be aware of how many sticks you have and where they are, so you are never left stickless.

8 Some of these spins are very easy, some can be more difficult, but as long as you "stick to it", you can master any or all of them…it's up to you.

9 Remember the more you drop your sticks, the better you'll get…as long as you keep picking them up and trying again.

10 I feel it important to mention, if only as "food for thought", that we the drummers of the world have an impact on the "consumption" of wood ; not only our sticks, but our drums as well, which means cutting down trees, which means less air to breathe…we could at least make sure we're replanting the ones we use. Food for thought.

WARMING UP

As with any physical exercise, warming up is always important. Be sure that before playing or spinning you do some light stretching, first without the sticks and then with them.

A pulled ligament or strained muscle can take weeks to heal, so be wise…warm up!

The following are some ideas for stretching, etc. that you can do to help prepare your body to perform efficiently. Of course these are just a few suggestions/examples, and you will find what works best for you by experimenting.

WITHOUT THE STICKS

1 Rub your hands together vigorously until they are hot.

2 Shake your hands as if you were trying to get water off of them.

3 Do "Windmills" (circles) with your arms, first FORWARD, then REVERSE.

4 Clasp your hands together behind your lower back, then bend forward, bringing the hands above your head.

5 Do "Squat Thrust". **a** First stand, then squat down (hands on the floor). **b** Kick your legs out behind you. **c** Do a push-up (or several, depending on your capability). **d** Bring your legs back in. **e** Stand and repeat.

6 Do push-ups on your fingertips. Be careful when you first start doing this, slowly building up your strength.

WITH THE STICKS

1 Roll two sticks around each other in one hand.

2 With a stick in each hand, turn the wrist from one side to the other (as in Chapter 1, #10).

3 Holding both ENDS in a fist (i.e., two sticks in one hand) turn your wrist from side to side (as in Chapter 2, #62).

4 With the stick held in FAKE GRIP go back and forth in A then go FORWARD OVER the 2nd finger into B, back and forth, then go FORWARD OVER the 3rd finger into C, back and forth, etc. (like Chapter 2, #1).

5 Play on a drum or practice pad some rudiments: Long Roll, Single Stroke Roll, 5-7-9-10-11-13-15 Stroke Rolls, Buzz Roll, Paradiddle, Flam, Flam Tap, Flamaque, Ruff, Triplets, etc. You should know all 26 standard drum rudiments. A great warm up is to start playing very slowly, then with each hit increase the tempo (like a train speeding up) until you reach a comfortable speed (still playing with relaxed and good technique), then slow down as gradually as you sped up until you are again going very slow.

PART TWO

SPINNING

THE BASIC SPINS

The following are the fifteen primary drumstick spins. They will serve as your "alphabet" for the following chapters. Each one represents a different category of spin.

1 GRIP SPIN
From READY POSITION spin the stick CLOCKWISE by turning the wrist, as if drawing a CLOCKWISE circle on the ground with the END of the stick.

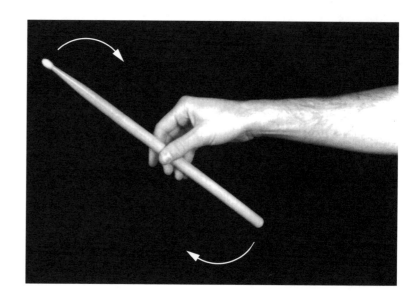

2 FAKE SPIN
Start in FAKE GRIP, open the hand as if shaking hands, and spin a REVERSE circle on both sides of the hand by working the 1st and 2nd fingers back and forth.

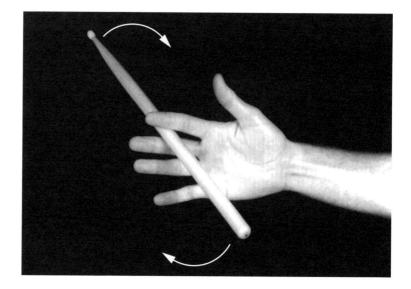

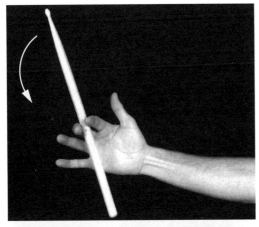

1

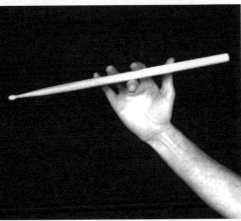

2

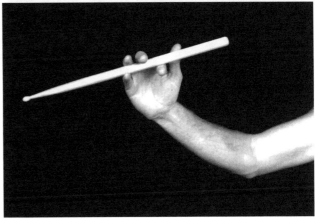

3

4

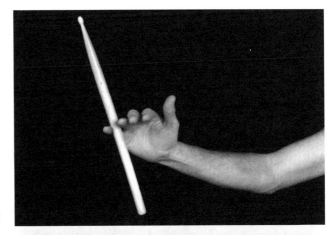

5

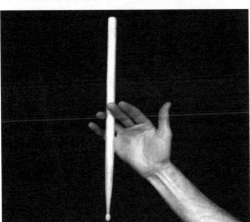

6

3 FORWARD SPIN

Begin with the stick in FAKE GRIP. From A/Y, spin
FORWARD (ph.1) OVER the 2nd finger, grabbing
with the 3rd finger (ph.2), let go with the 1st finger,
the stick is now in B (ph.3). Continue OVER the
3rd finger and grab with the 4th finger (ph.4), let go
with the 2nd finger, now the stick is in C (ph.5).
Continue FORWARD UNDER 3rd and 2nd fingers,
grabbing with the 1st finger (ph.6), let go with the
4th finger and you're back in A (the END is now
UP) repeat once again and the TIP will be UP.

4 PALM SPIN

From READY POSITION, PALM UP, turn the wrist COUNTERCLOCKWISE, then FLIP the stick while opening your hand so that it spins one revolution CLOCKWISE around the PALM, then close the fingers around the stick and you're back in READY POSITION.

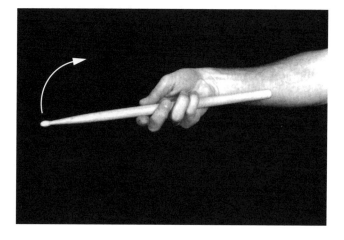
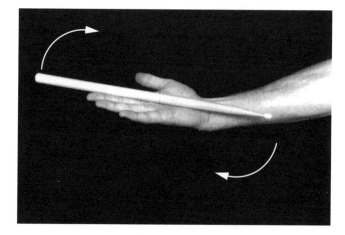

5 THUMB SPIN

Start in READY POSITION and FLIP the stick REVERSE so it spins around Y of the thumb one time, then back to READY POSITION.

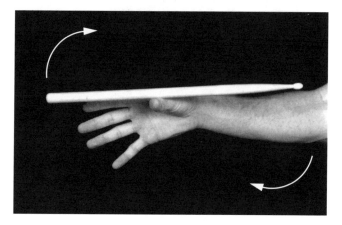

6 EXCHANGING STICKS

Start in READY POSITION, throw the right stick to the left hand while throwing the left stick to the right hand; the right stick passes in front of the left so that they don't collide. (no picture)

7 SINGLE TURN

From READY POSITION, grab the stick with Y/O of the 2nd finger and FLIP it REVERSE one full revolution by letting it roll OVER the 1st finger and back into READY POSITION.

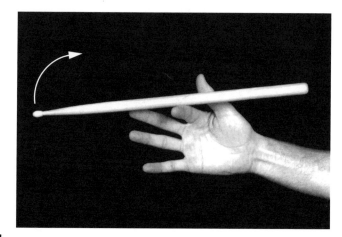

8 FIGURE EIGHT

Hold the stick in FAKE TRADITIONAL GRIP (ph. 1). Let the TIP drop FORWARD (ph. 2) then circle around to the right, back up, then down to the left (ph.3) and back up to the beginning (ph. 4), in a figure eight pattern.

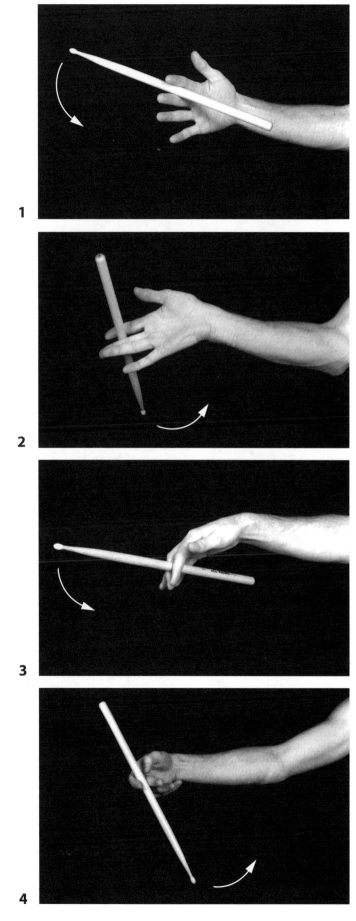

1

2

3

4

9 ROLL OVER ALL FOUR FINGERS

Holding the stick at the GRIP, turn the TIP slightly down and to the left (ph.1), then FLIP the stick so that it rolls CLOCKWISE OVER fingers 1,2,3, & 4, around S (ph.2), and grab it with your hand at the SHAFT (ph.3). Turn the wrist so your thumb points UP (ph.4). Now FLIP the stick so it spins REVERSE OVER fingers 4,3,2, & 1(ph.5)into G.

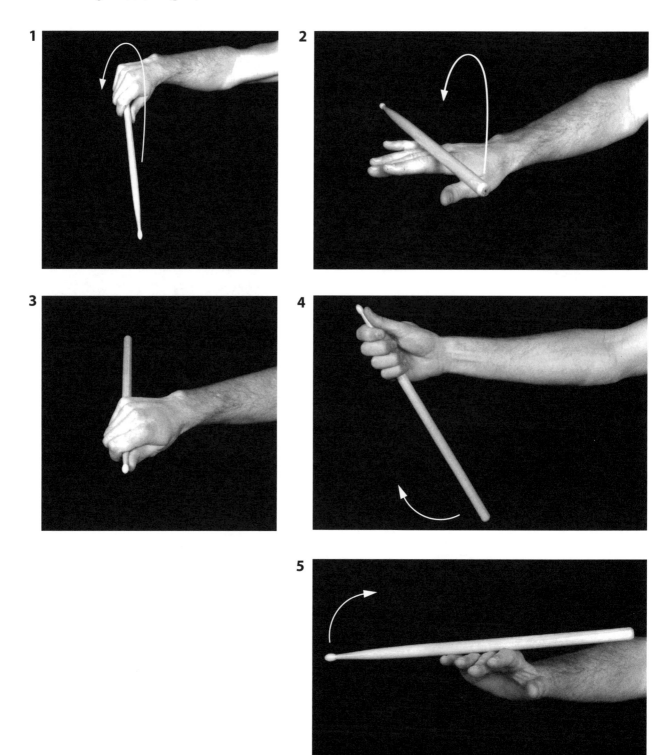

10 SIDE TO SIDE

Start in READY POSITION, and
turn the wrist from side to side
(no picture).
Note This is a great way to warm up
before playing or spinning
(see "Warming Up").

11   FIRST FINGERS ONLY

Using one stick with both hands,
place the stick between 1st fingers
in Y at the MIDDLE of the stick.
Spin FORWARD by moving the
fingers around each other in a
small forward circle.

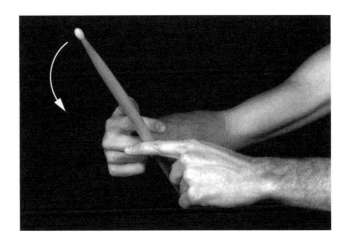

12 TOSSING

From READY POSITION toss
the stick up in the air one
full revolution in REVERSE
direction, then catch it in READY
POSITION(no picture).

13 E-"X"-HIBIT

(2 sticks, 1 hand)

Start with two sticks in one hand held UNDER 1st and 4th fingers, and OVER 2nd and 3rd (in Y and X) with P UP (ph. 1). Raising your arm UP and IN, let go with the 4th finger (ph. 2) while turning the wrist to the left so that P faces DOWN and grab the sticks OVER the 3rd finger (now held OVER 1st and 3rd fingers, and UNDER 2nd)(ph. 3). Close the hand into a fist, while jamming the TH between the sticks to make an "X"with both TIPS UP, held in B (ph.4).

Note This is a difficult spin and requires momentum to perform correctly. The best way to learn it is to use the other hand to walk through it and the best way to practice it is quickly, unlike the other spins where "slowly but surely" is the way to success.

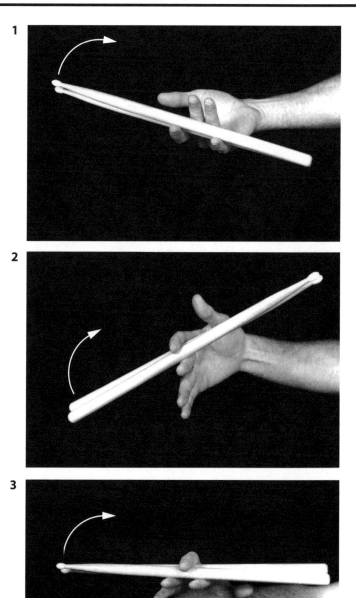

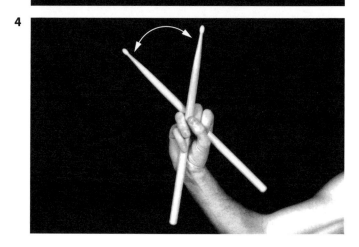

14 SWITCHING

(1 stick, 2 hands)
Right A   Left A
Start with the stick in right hand held
in FAKE GRIP. Spin FORWARD 1/2
revolution and grab the stick with A of L
(END is UP). Continue FORWARD, and
after 1/2 revolution grab it with A of R
and switch back and forth.

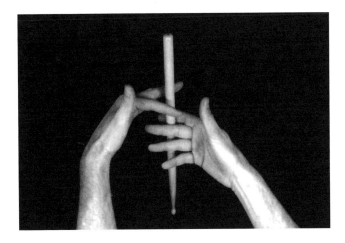

15 BALANCING THE STICK

From READY POSITION, open fingers so
that the stick only touches the 1st finger
and find the balance point. This will help
you gain better control of the stick.

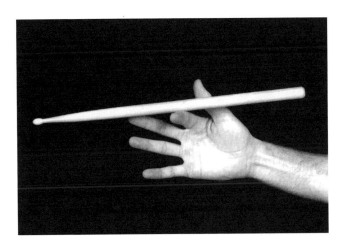

VARIATIONS

Using the 15 basic spins from chapter 1, you can now start to apply mathematical combinations and creativity to develop stick spinning. Here are some ideas to start you out.

1 BACK AND FORTH

From FAKE GRIP spin the stick FORWARD then REVERSE in A. After several times, go FORWARD OVER 2nd finger into B and continue back and forth movement. Then go FORWARD OVER 3rd finger into C and resume back and forth movement.
Note Not only is this a great warm-up exercise, but also an excellent way to develop a smooth transition from one SLOT to another.

2 FORWARD SPIN A-B-C, PALM FACING FRONT

Spin FORWARD SPIN (Chapter 1, #3) with P facing FRONT.

3 FORWARD SPIN A-B-C-A-B-C-G, PALM FACING FRONT

From FAKE GRIP do the FORWARD SPIN (Chapter 1,#3) with P facing FRONT. After spinning the pattern A-B-C, A-B-C go from C UNDER 3rd, 2nd, and 1st fingers back to READY POSITION.
Note You can move your arms out while doing this spin.

4 FORWARD SPIN A-B-C-B

From FAKE GRIP go FORWARD OVER 2nd finger into B, OVER 3rd finger into C, then go UNDER 3rd finger back into B, UNDER 2nd finger into A and continue or stop in FAKE GRIP.

5 FORWARD SPIN G-A-B-A

From READY POSTION, FLIP the stick FORWARD OVER 1st finger into A, OVER 2nd finger into B, then UNDER 2nd finger into A, UNDER 1st finger into G, and either stop or repeat.

6 FORWARD SPIN G-A-B-C-B-A-G

From READY POSITION, FLIP the stick FORWARD OVER 1st finger into A, OVER 2nd finger into B, OVER 3rd finger into C, then Under 3nd finger into B, UNDER 2nd finger into A, then UNDER 1st finger into G and you're back in READY POSITION.
Note This spin is best done one time only.

7 FORWARD SPIN G-A-B-C-B-A / G-A-B-A

Same as above (Chapter 2, #6) and then add to it Chapter 2, #5.

8 FORWARD SPIN A-B-C-B-C-B-A-B

From FAKE GRIP go FORWARD OVER 2nd finger into B, OVER 3rd finger into C, UNDER 3rd finger into B, OVER 3rd finger back into C, UNDER 3rd finger into B, UNDER 2nd finger into A, OVER 2nd finger into B, UNDER 2nd finger into A and continue.

9 HELICOPTER

Start with the stick on the ground in FAKE GRIP with the fingers pointing DOWN.
Spin the regular FORWARD SPIN (Chapter 1, #3), and slowly fly the stick up like a helicopter taking off, by lifting your arm UP.
Note This isn't as hard as it sounds. The trick is keeping enough pressure on the stick so that it doesn't slip out of the fingers.

10 GYROSCOPE

Spinning the FORWARD SPIN (Chapter 1, #3), slowly turn the wrist to the left until the PALM faces DOWN, then slowly rotate the wrist back to the right until the PALM faces UP, and continue back and forth.

11 SWITCHING

(1 stick, 2 hands) Right A-B-A, Left A-B-A.
From FAKE GRIP spin the FORWARD SPIN pattern A-B-A (i.e. from A go FORWARD OVER 2nd finger into B then UNDER 2nd finger back into A), grab the stick with A of the opposite hand, continue the A-B-A pattern, switch hands again, and repeat the sequence.

12 SWITCHING (1 stick, 2 hands)
Right A-B-C-A, Left A-B-C-A

From FAKE GRIP spin the FORWARD SPIN (Chapter 1, #3) one time, and when the stick is back in A (end OUT), let the momentum carry the stick so that the TIP points UP. As the TIP gets to the top, grab the stick with A of the other hand in FAKE GRIP and continue the FORWARD SPIN, then switch back and forth between your hands.

13 SWITCHING (1 stick, 2 hands)
Right A-B-C-B-A, Left A-B-C-B-A

From FAKE GRIP, spin the FORWARD SPIN A-B-C-B-A (Chapter 2, #4) and after A, switch to A of L (continuing the same pattern) and switch back and forth.

14 SWITCHING (1 stick, 2 hands)
Right C-B-A, Left C-B-A

Start in FAKE GRIP and spin FORWARD SPIN pattern A-B-C-A (Chapter 1, #3). Grab the stick with C of the opposite hand and continue FORWARD C-B-A pattern by going from C UNDER 3rd finger into B, UNDER 2nd finger into A, then grab the stick with C of the opposite hand and continue.

15 SWITCHING (1 stick, 2 hands)
Right A-C-A, Left A-C-A

From FAKE GRIP, spin FORWARD from A OVER 2nd and 3rd fingers into C, then UNDER 3rd and 2nd fingers into A, then grab the stick with the opposite hand in A and continue the A-C-A pattern, switch hands again and continue.

16 WALKING FORWARD
A-B repeated, C one time
From FAKE GRIP spin FORWARD OVER 2nd finger into B, UNDER 2nd finger into A, and repeat A-B-A-B until the hand is very near either end of the stick. Then from B go over 3rd finger into C, UNDER 3rd and 2nd fingers into A and continue the A-B-A pattern until your hand reaches the other end of the stick. Then by going through C one time, you will again reverse the direction that your hand "walks".

17 WALKING FORWARD
A one time, B-C repeated
Same as above (Chapter 2, #16) but this time after A, repeat the B-C pattern (FORWARD) until the hand reaches the end of the stick, then from C go UNDER 3rd & 2nd fingers into A, OVER 2nd finger into B and repeat the B-C pattern.

18 WALKING FORWARD
A-C repeated, B one time
Same as above (Chapter 2 #16 & 17) but now repeat A-C pattern by going from A, FORWARD OVER 2nd and 3rd fingers into C, then UNDER 3rd and 2nd fingers into A. Continue the A-C pattern and when the hand reaches the end of the stick, go into B either from A (going OVER 2nd finger) or from C (going UNDER 3rd finger), and continue the A-C pattern.

19 FORWARD SPIN
1 stick in each hand A-B-C FORWARD INTO "X" SHAPE
While spinning the FORWARD SPIN (Chapter 1, #3) gradually turn the hands IN intertwining the sticks. After several revolutions stop the sticks TIP UP so they cross in an "X" shape.
Note To avoid striking the sticks together, spin one stick slightly faster than the other to off-set them.

20 REVERSE SPIN A-B-C
From READY POSITION spin the stick in REVERSE direction by reaching behind the stick with the 2nd finger (O/Y), let go with TH and now it's in A with the end OUT. Reach behind the stick with the 3rd finger (O/Y), let go with 1st finger, and it's now in B. Then reach behind the stick with the 4th finger (O/Y), let go with the 2nd finger and now the stick is in C. To continue, the stick will go OVER 3rd and 2nd fingers, grab with 1st finger (P/Y), let go with the 4th finger and now the stick is back in A with the TIP OUT. Repeat or …
Stop the spin after C by letting the stick go OVER 3rd, 2nd and 1st fingers back into READY POSITION.

21 REVERSE SPIN A-B-C-B
As above (Chapter 2, #20), go in REVERSE direction from READY POSITION, spin UNDER 1st finger into A, UNDER 2nd finger into B, UNDER 3rd finger into C, then go OVER 3rd finger into B, OVER 2nd finger into A, and continue.

22 REVERSE SPIN A-B-C-B-A-G
As above (Chapter 2, #21) but this time after spinning the A-B-C-B-A pattern, go OVER the 1st finger into G and stop in READY POSITION. You can raise your arm as you do this spin so that when you're back to READY POSITION your arm is extended all the way up.
Note This spin is not so easily repeated. It is best done once. However if repeated, start from the MIDDLE of the stick and after two cycles your hand will be at the GRIP of the stick.

23 REVERSE SPIN A-B-C-B-C-B-A-B

As the preceding spins, (Chapter 2, #20,21,22) spin REVERSE spin from READY POSITION by grabbing the stick with 2nd finger (O/Y) into A, then UNDER 2nd finger into B, UNDER 3rd finger into C, OVER 3rd finger into B, (pay attention here) UNDER 3rd finger into C, OVER 3rd finger into B (for the second time), OVER 2nd finger into A, UNDER 2nd finger into B, OVER 2nd into A, and repeat or finish the spin by rolling OVER 1st finger into READY POSITION.

24 REVERSE SPIN C-B-A-G

From READY POSITION grab the stick with the 4th finger (Y/O) into C, and spin in REVERSE direction from C OVER 3rd finger into B, OVER 2nd finger into A, then let the stick spin OVER 1st finger back into READY POSITION.

Note This is also a good move to raise your arm up while spinning.

25 WALKING REVERSE
A-B repeated, C one time

From READY POSITION grab the stick with the 2nd finger (Y/O) and spin in REVERSE direction from A UNDER 2nd finger into B, OVER 2nd finger back into A and continue A-B pattern until your hand is near the end of the stick. Then from B go UNDER 3rd finger into C, OVER 3rd & 2nd fingers into A, UNDER 2nd finger into B, and resume the A-B pattern. Continue.

26 WALKING REVERSE
A one time, B-C repeated

As above (Chapter 2, #25) from READY POSITION (going in REVERSE direction) grab the stick with the 2nd finger (Y/O) into A, go UNDER the 2nd finger into B, UNDER 3rd finger into C, then OVER 3rd finger into B and continue the B-C pattern. When the hand reaches the end of the stick, go from C OVER 3rd & 2nd fingers into A, UNDER 2nd finger into B, UNDER 3rd finger into C, and continue the B-C pattern.

27 SIMULTANEOUS

Do the following spins by spinning each stick in different or opposite directions.

1 Right: A-B-C FORWARD (Chapter 1, #3)
   Left: A-B-C REVERSE (Chapter 2, #20)
2 Right: A-B-C REVERSE (Chapter 2, #20)
   Left: A-B-C FORWARD (Chapter 1, #3)
3 Right: A-B-C-B FORWARD (Chapter 2,#4)
   Left: A-B-C-B REVERSE (Chapter 2,#21)
4 Right: A-B-C-B REVERSE (Chapter 2,#21)
   Left: A-B-C-B FORWARD (Chapter 2, #4)

Note Once again I point out that the mathematical possibilities are virtually endless, as well as the creative application of these spins. Search and you shall find.

28 FORWARD FAKE SPIN

Start in FAKE GRIP (in knuckle Y or Z, whichever you prefer) with the hand opened so that P faces left and spin the stick FORWARD as if drawing forward circles on either side of the hand by working the 1st and 2nd fingers back and forth.

29 FORWARD FAKE SPIN A-B-C

Start in FAKE GRIP and do the FORWARD FAKE SPIN (Chapter 2, #28), this time in knuckle Y. After several revolutions spin the stick OVER the 2nd finger into B and continue the FORWARD FAKE SPIN. Then spin the stick OVER the 3rd finger into C, continue the FORWARD FAKE SPIN. Then go UNDER 3rd and 2nd fingers back into A (with the END now facing OUT). Continue this pattern.

Note You are combining the FORWARD FAKE SPIN (Chapter 2, #28) with the FORWARD SPIN (Chapter 1, #3).

30 FORWARD FAKE SPIN A-B-C-B

Using the FORWARD FAKE SPIN (Chapter 2, #28) go FORWARD from A, OVER 2nd finger into B, OVER 3rd finger into C, UNDER 3rd finger into B, UNDER 2nd finger into A, and repeat.

31 FORWARD FAKE SPIN A-C

From FAKE GRIP POSITION, with the stick in knuckle Z, and held at the ANKLE, spin the FORWARD FAKE SPIN (Chapter 2, #28) then spin the stick FORWARD OVER 2nd and 3rd fingers into C, then the stick goes UNDER 3rd and 2nd fingers into A and continue. To stop you can go from C UNDER 3rd, 2nd and 1st fingers back into READY POSITION.

Note If you do only one revolution of the FORWARD FAKE SPIN the stick will do WALKING. So you can either start from the ANKLE and after A-C-A the stick will be in READY POSITION, or do a few revolutions of the FORWARD FAKE SPIN each time to find your center of balance.

32 FORWARD FAKE SPIN / P FACING FRONT

Spin the FORWARD FAKE SPIN (Chapter 2, #28) but turn the hand so that the PALM is facing FRONT.

33 FORWARD FAKE (LEFT HAND)

Start in TRADITONAL GRIP (L). While turning the wrist so that P faces FRONT, spin the FORWARD FAKE SPIN (Chapter 2, #28) in B. To stop, turn the wrist back to TRADITIONAL GRIP and let the TIP follow through.

34 FORWARD FAKE SPIN /
WALKING A-B repeated, C one time

From FAKE GRIP, do the FORWARD FAKE SPIN (Chapter 2, #28), then go OVER 2nd finger into B, UNDER 2nd finger into A, and continue the A-B pattern. When the hand gets near the end of the stick, go from B OVER 3rd finger into C, then UNDER 3rd and 2nd fingers back into A, and continue the A-B pattern.

35 FORWARD FAKE SPIN/KNUCKLE Y TO Z

Practice spinning the FORWARD FAKE SPIN (Chapter 2, #28) and move the stick up and down from knuckle Y to knuckle Z by slightly loosening the grip of the fingers.

Note You can also do this spin in knuckle X, but of course it's more risky.

36 FAKE SPIN A-B-C

From FAKE GRIP spin a FAKE SPIN (Chapter 1, #2), then go in REVERSE direction UNDER 2nd finger into B, continue FAKE SPIN, go UNDER 3rd finger into C, continue FAKE SPIN, go OVER 3rd and 2nd fingers back to A, and repeat, or from A let the stick roll OVER 1st finger (in REVERSE direction) and back into READY POSITION.

37 FAKE SPIN A-B-C-B

As above (Chapter 2, #36) spin the FAKE SPIN (Chapter 1, #2) in A. Then spin the stick UNDER 2nd finger into B and continue the FAKE SPIN. Go UNDER 3rd finger into C, continue FAKE SPIN, go OVER 3rd finger into B, continue FAKE SPIN, and finally OVER 2nd finger back into A and repeat.

38 FAKE SPIN / TOSS

From FAKE GRIP spin the FAKE SPIN (Chapter 1, #2) and let the stick gradually slide toward the END by slightly loosening the grip of the fingers. When it finally reaches the ANKLE, TOSS (Chapter 1, #12) it up and catch it in READY POSITION.

39 FAKE SPIN in A / REVERSE SPIN B-C-B

This spin combines the FAKE SPIN (Chapter 1, #2) with the REVERSE SPIN (Chapter 2, #21). Start by spinning the FAKE SPIN, then spin the stick in REVERSE direction UNDER the 2nd finger into B, UNDER the 3rd finger into C, OVER the 3rd finger into B, OVER the 2nd finger into A, and resume the FAKE SPIN. Repeat.

40 FAKE SPIN / FORWARD FAKE SPIN

Start in the FAKE GRIP and spin the FAKE SPIN (Chapter 1, #2). Stop the stick in FAKE TRADITIONAL GRIP by turning the wrist to the right (so that P is now UP), turn the wrist back and spin the FORWARD FAKE SPIN (Chapter 2, #28), then stop in FAKE GRIP and repeat.

41 MOVING THE ARM A-B-C-B-A

Move your arm to the FRONT when the stick spins FORWARD, and BACK when spinning in REVERSE direction. From FAKE GRIP, spin FORWARD OVER the 2nd finger into B, OVER the 3rd finger into C, then REVERSE OVER the 3rd finger into B, over the 2nd finger into A, and continue while moving the arm.

42 MOVING THE ARM A-B-A-C-G

From FAKE GRIP spin the stick FORWARD OVER 2nd finger into B, then REVERSE back OVER 2nd finger into A, then go FORWARD OVER 2nd and 3rd fingers into C. From there spin the stick in REVERSE direction OVER 3rd, 2nd, and 1st fingers into READY POSITION. As in Chapter 2, #41, move the arm with the stick.

43 MOVING THE ARM A-C-A

From FAKE GRIP spin the stick FORWARD OVER 2nd and 3rd fingers into C, then REVERSE OVER 3rd and 2nd fingers returning to A. Continue back and forth. As in Chapter 2, #41, move the arm with the stick.

44 MOVING THE ARM G-C-G

From ready position, FLIP the stick FORWARD OVER 1st, 2nd, and 3rd fingers into C, then REVERSE OVER 3rd, 2nd, and 1st fingers back into READY POSITION. And again like Chapter 2, #41, you are moving the arm with the stick.

45 MOVING THE ARM A-B-A-C / TOSS

Using Chapter 2, #42 (A-B-A-C-G) when the stick is in C, TOSS it up in the air 1/2 revolution and catch it in READY POSITION. You can do this with any spin that has C in it.

46 FIGURE 8 A & B & C / FORWARD SPIN C-B-A

Start with FIGURE 8 (Chapter 1, #8) in A. After several repetitions, when the stick is on the outside of the hand, spin OVER 2nd finger into B, repeat FIGURE 8 pattern in B several times, then spin OVER 3rd finger into C, continuing FIGURE 8. Then using FORWARD SPIN (Chapter 2, #4 from C) spin FORWARD UNDER 3rd finger into B, UNDER 2nd finger into A, and resume the FIGURE 8.

47 FIGURE 8 REVERSE SIDEWAYS A-B-C / FORWARD SPIN C-B-A

After spinning the FIGURE 8 pattern, stop the stick in FAKE TRADITIONAL GRIP. While turning the wrist to the left, spin REVERSE SIDEWAYS (see "Directions") from A UNDER 2nd finger into B, and UNDER 3rd finger into C. Then do one FORWARD FAKE SPIN (Chapter 2, #28) to get the stick spinning FORWARD, and spin from C UNDER 3rd finger into B, UNDER 2nd finger into A, do FORWARD FAKE SPIN and resume FIGURE 8. Repeat.

48 FIGURE 8 TRADITIONAL GRIP

From TRADITIONAL GRIP the TIP end goes DOWN and OUT and continues in the FIGURE 8 (Chapter 1, #8) pattern.

49 THUMB SPIN COUNTERCLOCKWISE

Start with the stick in READY POSITION, then turn the wrist to the right so that P faces UP. Open the fingers and hold the stick with TH and 1st fingers (slightly resting on the 2nd, 3rd, and 4th fingers). With the 2nd finger FLIP the stick COUNTERCLOCKWISE (horizontal plane), so that it spins around the Y knuckle of TH and catch it in READY POSITION.

50 THUMB SPIN / ROLL OVER "O"

Start with the THUMB SPIN COUNTER-CLOCKWISE (Chapter 2, #49). As the stick spins around TH, turn the wrist to the left (P facing DOWN) and let the stick spin one time over O (back of the hand). Then it rolls around S and back into READY POSITION.
Note This is probably the most risky spin in the book.

51 THUMB SPIN FORWARD

From READY POSITION hold the stick back (as if you're about to hit the drum) and use the 2nd finger to FLIP the stick so that it spins FORWARD around TH and back into READY POSITION.

52 COUNTERCLOCKWISE A-B-C / FORWARD SPIN C-B-A

Start in FAKE GRIP and spin 1/2 revolution of the FORWARD FAKE SPIN (Chapter 2, #28), then spin COUNTERCLOCKWISE (vertical plane) UNDER 2nd finger into B, UNDER 3rd finger into C. Then do the FORWARD FAKE SPIN for 1/2 revolution, and continue FORWARD UNDER 3rd finger into B, UNDER 2nd finger into A, and repeat.
Note The FORWARD FAKE SPIN will help to change the direction in which the stick is spinning.

53 COUNTERCLOCKWISE A-B / FORWARD SPIN B-A

Same as above (Chapter 2, #52) but this time using A and B only. Start in FAKE GRIP, do 1/2 spin of FORWARD FAKE SPIN (Chapter 2, #28), then go COUNTERCLOCKWISE UNDER 2nd finger into B, do 1/2 revolution FORWARD FAKE SPIN (with END OUT) and go FORWARD UNDER 2nd finger into A. Repeat.

54 SIDEWAYS A-B-C / REVERSE C-B-A

Part 1 From FAKE TRADITIONAL GRIP spin the stick REVERSE SIDEWAYS while turning the wrist so that P faces left. From A go UNDER 2nd finger into B, then UNDER 3rd finger into C. Then do the FORWARD FAKE SPIN (Chapter 2, #28) until the TIP of the stick faces DOWN.
Part 2 Now spin REVERSE from C OVER 3rd finger into B, OVER 2nd finger into A, then do FAKE SPIN (Chapter 1, #2) one time and catch the stick between TH and 1st finger and it's back in FAKE TRADITIONAL GRIP. Repeat.

55 SIDEWAYS A-B-C / COUNTERCLOCKWISE C-B-A

As above (Chapter 2, #54) start from FAKE TRADITIONAL GRIP and spin the stick SIDEWAYS UNDER 2nd finger into B, UNDER 3rd finger into C (while turning the wrist and moving the arm OUT), do 1/2 spin of FORWARD FAKE SPIN (Chapter 2, #28) so that the TIP faces DOWN. Now spin COUNTERCLOCKWISE OVER 3rd finger into B, OVER 2nd finger into A, and catch the stick in FAKE GRIP. To continue, do one FAKE SPIN (Chapter 1, #2), stop in FAKE TRADITIONAL GRIP and repeat.

56 TOSS 1/2 TURN

From READY POSITION turn the wrist so that P faces left, then TOSS (Chapter 1, #12) the stick UP in REVERSE direction so it makes 1/2 revolution and catch it in READY POSITION (END OUT). Repeat.

57 TOSS (1 or more time)

To practice TOSSING (Chapter 1, #12), TOSS the stick UP 1 full spin, then 1 1/2, then 2, 2 1/2, 3, etc. up to 10 or more.

Note After 5 or 6 revolutions it becomes difficult to count, but you can "feel" how many times the stick spins. (For example, if you TOSS the stick a little higher than 7 revolutions it'll be 7 1/2). Try TOSSING the stick higher and slower (fewer revolutions) or lower and faster (more revolutions).

58 JUGGLING (3 sticks)

Start with two sticks in the right hand and one in the left, holding the sticks at the ANKLE. TOSS (Chapter 1, #12) one of the sticks in the right hand so that it turns one full revolution and lands in the left hand. Meanwhile, as that stick starts to fall (from its highest point), TOSS the stick in the left hand so it does one full revolution and lands in the right hand. Continue to throw left, then right, etc.

Note Once you start there will always be one stick in the air, one stick in your hand, and one stick being TOSSED.

59 TOSS CLOCKWISE / FORWARD FAKE SPIN

From READY POSITION turn the stick so that the TIP faces to the left and TOSS (Chapter 1, #12) the stick so that it spins one full revolution CLOCKWISE. While the stick is in the air, turn the wrist so that P faces UP and catch the stick in TRADITIONAL GRIP. Then spin the FORWARD FAKE SPIN (Chapter 2, #28) in B. To stop, when the TIP faces FRONT slide the 1st and 2nd fingers across the stick so that it's back in READY POSITION.

60 TOSS FORWARD

Holding the stick at the GRIP or ANKLE (whichever you prefer), TOSS (Chapter 1, #12) it UP so that it spins FORWARD one full revolution and catch in READY POSITION.

61 TOSS (Snatch out of the air)

TOSS the stick UP (Chapter 2, #57) at least 3 or 4 revolutions and catch it by thrusting your arm out quickly to snatch it out of the air.

Note If you miss it, the stick will hit your hand and will be knocked out into the audience, as if you meant to do that.

62 SIDE TO SIDE (2 sticks, 1 hand)

Close your hand making a fist, insert the END of both sticks into either end of the hand so that they slightly overlap inside the fist. Turn the wrist from side to side quickly to create the illusion of a spin. **Note** Although this isn't much for actual Spinology, it is a great warm-up exercise. Also, from a distance it can look impressive.

63 DROP FAKE

Holding the stick at the GRIP, let the TIP end drop FORWARD (while turning the wrist slightly to the right so that P faces UP) and circle around the outside of the hand, and then back up to the top. Repeat.

64 SINGLE TURN 1/2 REVOLUTION

From READY POSITION, FLIP the stick REVERSE 1/2 revolution by grabbing it with Y/O of the 2nd finger; now it's in A with the END facing the front. Move the 1st finger across the stick so it's back in READY POSITION (with the END out) and repeat.

65 2nd 3rd or 4th FINGERS ONLY (1 stick, 2 hands)

As Chapter 1, #11, spin the stick FORWARD by placing it between the 2nd fingers of both hands, in Y, and moving the fingers around each other in a small forward circle. Then you can go OVER 2nd finger of the right hand into B and continue spinning with the 3rd fingers. Then spin OVER 3rd finger into C, and continue with 4th fingers. **Note** This is a nice warm-up / stretching exercise for your fingers.

66 GRIP SPIN COUNTERCLOCKWISE

Do the same as Chapter 1, #1, this time as if drawing a COUNTERCLOCKWISE circle on the ground with the END of the stick.

67 EXCHANGING STICKS

As in Chapter 1, #6, throw the right stick to the left hand, and vice-versa, but this time the right stick goes behind the left stick.

68 FIGURE 8 IN GRIP POSITION

Do the FIGURE 8 (Chapter 1, #8), but this time held in GRIP POSITION.

69 FINGERTIPS

a Start in READY POSITION, then turn the wrist so that P faces UP. Using TH, 1st and 2nd fingers, spin the stick COUNTERCLOCKWISE (horizontal plane) from G to A to G etc., gradually sliding the stick up until it spins on top of TH, 1st, and 2nd fingers.
b (1 stick, 2 hands) Using both hands, spin FORWARD with the fingertips of TH, 1st and 2nd fingers.

70 ROLL OVER ALL FOUR FINGERS

From Chapter 1, #9, hold the stick in READY POSITION at the ANKLE; turn the wrist slightly to the left so that the TIP of the stick faces left. FLIP the stick to the right so that it rolls CLOCKWISE (vertical plane) OVER fingers 1, 2, 3, and 4, across S and back into READY POSITION (now the stick is held at the SHAFT). FLIP the stick COUNTERCLOCKWISE back OVER fingers 4, 3, 2, & 1 and repeat.

APPLICATION

Theoretically all of the spins in this book can be applied to live playing situations, or video filming. Here are some examples that I've found especially useful for performance. Use these spins before or after snare drum hits, cymbal crashes, etc., or if the song has a rest (for example, the guitar makes a two-bar fill before the solo), you can put in an appropriate spin to fill in the space. At the end of this chapter you'll find a page of rhythms that can be played with one hand. Practice with each hand individually and improvise spinning with the free hand.

As a warm up exercise play the following pattern: Strike the snare drum once each time you see the word HIT for the following spins.

a From FAKE GRIP, HIT the drum, then spin one revolution of the FAKE SPIN (Chapter 1, #2) while turning the wrist so that P faces UP.

b Stop the stick in FAKE TRADITIONAL GRIP, HIT, then spin one revolution of the FORWARD FAKE SPIN (Chapter 2, #28).

c Return to GRIP POSITION and HIT, then spin the SINGLE TURN 1/2 REVOLUTION (Chapter 2, #64).

d HIT, then spin the SINGLE TURN 1/2 REVOLUTION (Chapter 2, # 64) and repeat.

1 SINGLE TURN (Chapter 1, #7)
From READY POSITION, FLIP the stick REVERSE one full revolution by grabbing it with Y/O of the 2nd finger and letting it spin OVER the 1st finger and back into READY POSITION.

2 FAKE SPIN / FORWARD FAKE SPIN (Chapter 2, #40)
Start in FAKE GRIP and spin the FAKE SPIN (Chapter1, #2). Stop the stick in FAKE TRADITIONAL GRIP by turning the wrist to the right (so that P is now UP), then turn the wrist back and spin the FORWARD FAKE SPIN (Chapter 2, #28), stop in FAKE GRIP and continue.

3 GRIP SPIN (Chapter 1, #1)
From READY POSITION spin the stick CLOCKWISE by turning the wrist, as if drawing a CLOCKWISE circle on the ground with the END of the stick.

4 TOSS CLOCKWISE / FORWARD FAKE SPIN
(Chapter 2, #59) (R)
HI HAT PLAYING POSITION
From READY POSITION turn the stick so that
the TIP faces to the left and TOSS (Chapter 1,
#12) the stick so that it spins one full revolution
CLOCKWISE. While the stick is in the air, turn
the wrist so that P faces UP and catch the stick
in TRADITIONAL GRIP. Then spin a FORWARD
FAKE SPIN (Chapter 2, #28) in B.
To stop, when the TIP faces FRONT slide
the 1st and 2nd fingers across the stick so that it's
back in READY POSITION.

5 TOSS 1/2 TURN (Chapter 2, #56)
From READY POSITION TOSS (Chapter 1, #l2)
the stick UP in REVERSE direction so it makes 1/2
revolution and catch it in READY POSITION
(held at SHAFT). Repeat.

6 FAKE SPIN (Chapter 1, #2)
Start in FAKE GRIP and spin the stick as if drawing
a REVERSE circle on either side of the hand by
working the fingers back and forth.
Note For example you can raise your arm after
each snare hit while spinning the FAKE SPIN.

7 FAKE SPIN / A-B FORWARD
From FAKE GRIP (held at GRIP) spin one or two
revolutions of FAKE SPIN (Chapter 1, #2), then
stop in FAKE TRADITIONAL GRIP with the TIP
pointing UP. Now go FORWARD OVER 2nd finger
into B, then UNDER 2nd and 1st fingers back into
A and you're in READY POSITION.

8 TOSS CLOCKWISE
From HI HAT PLAYING POSITION TOSS
(Chapter 1 #12) the stick so that it spins one full
revolution CLOCKWISE and catch it in READY
POSITION.

9 FORWARD FAKE SPIN (with P facing BACK)
Spin the FORWARD FAKE SPIN (Chapter 2, #28)
with P facing BACK (see "Directions").

**10 FAKE SPIN / SIDEWAYS A-B-C / REVERSE
C-B-A**
From FAKE GRIP hit the drum, then spin several
revolutions of FAKE SPIN (Chapter 1, #2) and stop
in FAKE TRADITIONAL GRIP. Hit the drum again
and spin the SIDEWAYS A-B-C / REVERSE C-B-A
(Chapter 2, #54).

11 REVERSE SPIN G-A-B-C-B-A-G
(Chapter 2, #22)
From READY POSITION reach behind the stick
with the 2nd finger (O/Y) and spin REVERSE from
A, UNDER 2nd finger into B, under 3rd finger
into C, OVER 3rd finger into B, OVER 2nd finger
into A, and finally OVER 1st finger into READY
POSITION.

12 FIGURE 8 TRADITIONAL GRIP (LEFT HAND)
(Chapter 2, #48)
From TRADITIONAL GRIP the TIP end goes
DOWN and OUT and continues in the FIGURE 8
(Chapter 1, #8) pattern.

13 FAKE SPIN (off beat 8ths)
From HI HAT PLAYING POSITION, the right
hand plays off beat 8th notes on the hi hat (on all of
the "&'s") and spins one FAKE SPIN (Chapter 1, #2)
for each hit; meanwhile the left hand hits the snare
drum on beats two and four and after each hit spins
two or more (depending on the tempo of the song)
revolutions of the FAKE SPIN.

14 "X" CROSS
Hold the sticks together so that they cross in an "X"
pattern after each hit; or do E-"X"-HIBIT
(Chapter 1, #13) when you have a rest in the music.

15 EXCHANGING STICKS (Chapter 1, #6)
Start in READY POSITION, throw the right stick to the left hand while throwing the left stick to the right hand; the right stick passes in front of the left so that they don't collide.

16 TOSSING (Chapter 1, #12)
From READY POSITION throw the stick UP in the air one full revolution in REVERSE direction, then catch it in READY POSITION.

17 "X"- SWITCH STICKS
Hold the sticks up in an "X" (with the right stick on top of the left stick), then switch the sticks by raising left TH and sliding the right stick down (into G of the left hand). Meanwhile, the right hand slides up to the left stick, and into G. Pull the hands apart and you've switched the sticks into opposite hands.

18 HALF TOSS RIGHT / HALF TOSS LEFT
From MATCH GRIP and using the HI HAT PLAYING POSITION, TOSS (Chapter 1, #12) the right stick 1/2 revolution CLOCKWISE and catch it, then after the snare hit, TOSS the left stick REVERSE and catch it, and repeat.
Note You can try playing the hi hat with the left foot, instead of the right hand, to keep the time, thereby freeing your hands to spin.

19 HALF TOSS CLOCKWISE / HALF TOSS REVERSE (R only)
From HI HAT PLAYING POSITION, TOSS (Chapter1,#12) the right stick CLOCKWISE 1/2 revolution, catch it at the SHAFT, then turn your wrist so that the END points FRONT and TOSS it REVERSE 1/2 revolution so you're back in READY POSITION.

20 FAKE SPIN 1/4 NOTES HI HAT / 2 & 4 ON THE SNARE
Start by holding both sticks in FAKE GRIP (HI HAT PLAYING POSITION). Play 1/4 notes on the hi hat with R and spin one revolution of FAKE SPIN (Chapter 1, #2) for each hit. Play the snare drum on beats 2 & 4 with L and spin two revolutions of FAKE SPIN for each hit.

21 FROM CROSS STICK
There are several ways to switch from a rim shot (or cross stick) to the snare drum. Usually I do this: After the rim shot (left hand) turn L so that P faces UP and hit the snare with TRADITIONAL GRIP, then do one revolution of the FORWARD FAKE SPIN (Chapter 2, #28) (holding the stick in B) while turning the wrist so that P faces DOWN and slide the 1st & 2nd fingers over the stick so it's back in READY POSITION. Also try the SINGLE TURN 1/2 REVOLUTION (Chapter 2, #64).

22 RESTS
This isn't a spin, rather a suggestion. When a song has a rest in it, you can do some of the more difficult and flashy spins without worrying about losing the sound. If you play in a band that works or rehearses regularly, experiment with spins and tricks. By adding a spin here, a toss there, you can slowly come up with a tasty show, complete with solid drumming, nice stick spinning, and a smooth flow to the program.
A strong word of advice: keep your foot tapping, or count in your head, and somehow make sure that you don't lose your place in the song.

ONE HANDED RHYTHMS

The idea here is to be able to play a complete rhythm on the drum set with one hand, so that you train yourself to use the other hand for improvising. Basically any "linear" beat will work. Try these out, and then write out your own one handed rhythms.

Hi hat
Snare
Bass drum
Floor tom

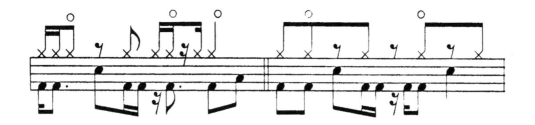

(Hip hop)

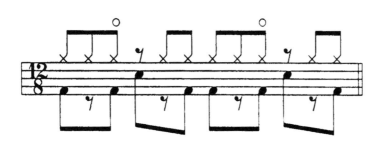

Hi Hat with foot

(Blues)

COMBINATIONS

1 a Start with both sticks held in FAKE GRIP and crossed in an "X". Spin the FAKE SPIN (Chapter 1, #2) with the PALMS facing BACK, while raising your arms UP and OUT. Stop in FAKE TRADITIONAL GRIP with P facing UP.

b From FAKE TRADITIONAL GRIP spin the sticks SIDEWAYS A-B-C/ COUNTERCLOCKWISE C-B-A (Chapter 2, #55), spin COUNTERCLOCKWISE C-B-A while moving arms IN, and stop the sticks in A (FAKE GRIP) so that they are parallel to each other in front of your face.

c With both sticks spin the FAKE SPIN (Chapter 1, #2) and move your hands in a REVERSE circle around each other.

d Stop the sticks in FAKE TRADITIONAL GRIP, crossed in an "X".

e Spin the FORWARD FAKE SPIN A-B-C (Chapter 2, #29) two times.

f Spin the FORWARD SPIN (Chapter 1, #3) and gradually turn the wrists toward each other so that the sticks intertwine (Chapter 2, #19) and stop, forming an "X".

2 a From FAKE GRIP spin the FORWARD SPIN (Chapter 1, #3) four times (i.e. A-B-C, A-B-C, A-B-C, A).

b From A , spin the FORWARD FAKE SPIN (Chapter 2, #28) two or three revolutions.

c Spin the FORWARD FAKE SPIN A-B-C (Chapter 2, #29) two times.

d Now do MOVING THE ARM A-B-A-C-G (Chapter 2, #42).

3 Refer to each spin from the various chapters.

a FIGURE 8 (Chapter 1, #8)

b FIGURE 8 REVERSE SIDEWAYS A-B-C / FORWARD SPIN C-B-A (Chapter 2, #47).

c FAKE SPIN (Chapter 1, # 2)

d REVERSE SPIN A-B-C-B (Chapter 2, #21)

e MOVING THE ARM A-B-A-C / TOSS (Chapter 2, #45)

4 a From MATCH GRIP , TOSS the right stick very high (4 or 5 spins). While it is in the air, pass the stick from L to R, and catch the stick from the air with L. Repeat this a few times.

b The last time you TOSS the stick up, quickly grab a third stick and juggle (Chapter 2, #58). When you want to finish juggling, throw the right stick very high, put the left stick down, and catch the falling stick with L.

c With R spin the FORWARD SPIN (Chapter 1,#3) and with L spin the REVERSE SPIN A-B-C (Chapter 2, #20). [Like doing Chapter 2, #27-1].

d Put one stick down, and go into SWITCHING (Chapter 2, #11). Repeat several times.

e When the stick is in R and in A, do the FIGURE 8 (Chapter 1, #8), and simultaneously pick up the other stick and do the FIGURE 8 with L.

f Do the FIGURE 8 REVERSE SIDEWAYS A-B-C/ FORWARD C-B-A (Chapter 2, #47).

5 a Do WALKING FORWARD A-B repeated, C one time (Chapter 2, #16)

b FAKE SPIN / TOSS (Chapter 2, #38)

c Roll OVER ALL FOUR FINGERS (Chapter 2, #70)

d Toss 1, 1½, 2, etc. (Chapter 2, #57)

e FAKE SPIN (Chapter 1, #2)

f Sideways A-B-C / REVERSE C-B-A (Chapter 2, #54)

g COUNTERCLOCKWISE A-B-C / FORWARD SPIN C-B-A (Chapter 2, #52)

h COUNTERCLOCKWISE A-B / FORWARD SPIN B-A, (Chapter 2, #53)

i FORWARD SPIN G-A-B-A (Chapter 2, #5)

j Fingertips (Chapter 2, #69)

k Exchange sticks (Chapter 1, #6)

6

a Thumb spin (Chapter 1, #5)

b Thumb spin COUNTERCLOCKWISE (Chapter 2, #49)

c Thumb spin / ROLL OVER "O" (Chapter 2, #50)

d Helicopter (if missed from above) (Chapter 2, #9)

e Grip spin (Chapter 1, #1)

f Thumb spin FORWARD (Chapter 2, #51)

g TOSS FORWARD (Chapter 2, #60)

h TOSS (Chapter 1, #12)

i TOSS Snatch out of air (Chapter 2, #61)

7

a Toss CLOCKWISE / FORWARD FAKE (Chapter 2, #59)

b Figure 8, in A & B & C / FORWARD SPIN C-B-A (Chapter 2, #46)

c Figure 8 REVERSE SIDEWAYS A-B-C / FORWARD SPIN C-B-A (Chapter 2, #47)

d Improvise, using Chapter 2, #1 any pattern .

e Moving arm A-B-A-C / TOSS (Chapter 2, #45)

HUMOR

Here are some ideas for your entertainment, amusement, and imagination to further inspire your creativity with the drumsticks.

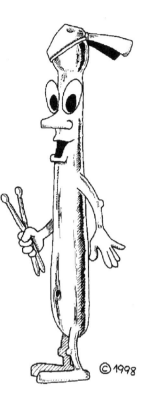

Balance the stick in the center of your palm.

Use the stick to scratch your back.

Use the stick as a "shoe horn" by putting the TIP end of the stick in the back of your shoes to help fit them on your feet.

Use the stick to tuck in your shirt.

Use the sticks for rolling dough when making bread.

Write your name in the sand.

Tie fishing line just below the TIP, attach a hook, bait it, and go catch a fish.

If you're ever attacked by an alligator, you can prop its mouth open with the stick and run!

Use the stick to turn off light switches, push the elevator button, move wires, touch cords, and basically deal with electricity safely without being shocked.

Use a stick as a "foot in the door" for catching doors and elevators before they close.

As in the circus, balance plates, balls etc. on either end of the stick.

Use the END of the stick to pulverize vitamins, seasoning, spices etc. in your favorite kitchen bowl.

When opening soft drinks in aluminum cans, push the end of the stick against the middle of the tab thus enabling you to open the can easier.

With a stick held in each hand, flap your arms excessively fast and fly!

Try chapter 2 #9 (Helicopter) if you ever need to go up quickly!

Use the stick as a "belt" if your pants are too big, by putting a stick through two or more of the loops on your pants to take up the slack.

Use the stick to help press adhesive tape or stickers flat, thus adhering better (get it, so they STICK better).

Use the stick as a black board/map pointer.

Mark your stick in inches (or centimeters) and use it as a measure / ruler.

Use the stick as a straight edge to draw or mark a straight line, remembering of course that the stick tapers off toward the TIP end.

Use the stick as a "comparative tape measure" to compare sizes, spaces etc.
Ex: A piece of furniture 4 1/2 sticks wide, will fit in a hallway that is 5 sticks wide.

Use the stick as a "pry bar" or for leverage when moving small or medium sized objects.
Ex: If you have to lift a wooden crate, you can put the TIP end under it first to help you get a grip with your fingers.

Use the sticks as a "wrench" by putting "wing nuts" between them; a) grab the sticks at either end, applying enough pressure to keep them from slipping off, b)turn the wing nut to either tighten or loosen it.

Make a "splint" for broken arms, propping up small trees or branches, helping wounded animals, etc.

Hold your sticks next to a tree and say "MAMA".

Stir paint with the stick.

Use the stick to find water.

Use the sticks to play "fetch" with your dog.

Use the stick as a putter to play golf.

Play Baseball holding the TIP end and hit the ball with the END.

Play billiards.

Hold the stick at the TIP end and throw it into the grass or sand so that it stands up by itself.

Toss your salad with the drumsticks.

Use old sticks as kindling in your fireplace.

Rub two sticks together very fast and start a fire.

Use the END of the stick to pry off bottle tops.

When you're eating at a restaurant and the table wobbles a little, you can put a stick under one leg, and voila, it's steady.

Knock on doors (rat-a tat-tat) thus saving your fingers/knuckles for playing and spinning.

Conductor's baton; Hold the stick at the END and conduct an orchestra.
In Common time or (4/4) beat one is down, beat two to the left, beat three to the right, and beat four is back up.

Give a stick to your guitarist to use as a "slide".

Play the violin.

Foot Massage: With both sticks side by side on the floor, roll your feet back and forth over them, thus stimulating the nerve endings in your feet. Now try it with several sticks on the floor.

Rubber pencil: from GRIP POSITION jostle the stick by moving the wrist up and down, to create the effect that the stick is made of rubber.

Use the sticks as "chop sticks" or "tongs" to grab things. For example if you drop a hairbrush behind the washing machine, you could get it with the sticks.

Suspending the stick. Start by holding the stick in READY POSITION with your arm extended in front of you. Raise your arm UP, and open the fingers letting the stick fall. As the stick starts to drop catch it by lowering the arm quickly, raise it UP again and repeat.

Carry your knapsack, pouch, etc. by holding the stick over one shoulder and attaching the bag to the other end of it.

AT A GLANCE

Chapter One : The Basic Spins

1 BACK AND FORTH

FORWARD SPIN

2 A-B-C, P FRONT

3 A-B-C-A-B-C-G, P FRONT

4 A-B-C-B

5 G-A-B-A

6 G-A-B-C-B-A-G

7 G-A-B-C-B-A / G-A-B-A

8 A-B-C-B-C-B-A-B

9 HELICOPTER

10 GYROSCOPE

SWITCHING

11 R A-B-A L A-B-A

12 R A-B-C-A L A-B-C-A

13 R A-B-C-B-A L A-B-C-B-A

14 R C-B-A L C-B-A

15 R A-C-A L A-C-A

WALKING FORWARD

16 A-B repeated, C one time

17 A one time, B-C repeated

18 A-C repeated, B one time

19 FORWARD SPIN A-B-C FORWARD into "X" SHAPE

REVERSE SPIN

20 A-B-C

21 A-B-C-B

22 A-B-C-B-A-G

23 A-B-C-B-C-B-A-B

24 C-B-A-G

WALKING REVERSE

25 A-B repeated, C one time

26 A one time, B-C repeated

27 SIMULTANEOUS

28 FORWARD FAKE SPIN

29 A-B-C

30 A-B-C-B

31 A-C

32 P FRONT

33 L(Traditional grip)

34 WALKING A-B repeated, C one time

35 KNUCKLE Y TO Z

FAKE SPIN

36 A-B-C

37 A-B-C-B

38 TOSS

39 in A / REVERSE SPIN B-C-B

40 / FORWARD FAKE SPIN

MOVING THE ARM

41 A-B-C-B-A

42 A-B-A-C-G

43 A-C-A

44 G-C-G

45 A-B-A-C / TOSS

FIGURE 8

46 Figure 8 A&B&C / FORWARD SPIN C-B-A

47 Figure 8 REVERSE SIDEWAYS A-B-C / FORWARD SPIN C-B-A

48 Figure 8 TRADITIONAL

49 THUMB SPIN COUNTER CLOCKWISE

50 THUMB SPIN / ROLL OVER "O"

51 THUMB SPIN FORWARD

1 SINGLE TURN (Chapter 1, #7)

2 FAKE SPIN / FORWARD FAKE SPIN (Ch. 2, #40)

3 GRIP SPIN (Chapter 1, #1)

4 TOSS CLOCKWISE / FORWARD FAKE SPIN (Ch.2, #59)

5 TOSS 1/2 TURN (Chapter 2, #56)

6 FAKE SPIN (Chapter l, #2)

7 FAKE SPIN / A-B FORWARD

8 TOSS CLOCKWISE

9 FORWARD FAKE SPIN (with P facing BACK)

10 FAKE SPIN / SIDEWAYS A-B-C / REVERSE C-B-A

11 REVERSE SPIN G-A-B-C-B-A-G (Ch. 2, #22)

12 FIGURE 8 TRADITIONAL GRIP (L) (Ch. 2, #48)

13 FAKE SPIN (off beat 8ths)

14 "X" CROSS

15 EXCHANGING STICKS (Ch. 1, #6)

16 TOSSING (Ch. 1, #12)

17 "X"- SWITCH STICKS

18 HALF TOSS RIGHT / HALF TOSS LEFT

19 HALF TOSS CLOCKWISE / HALF TOSS REVERSE (R only)

20 FAKE SPIN: 1/4 NOTES HI HAT / 2 & 4 SNARE

21 FROM CROSS STICK

22 RESTS

1 a FAKE (Chapter 1, #2)

b (Chapter 2, #55)

c FAKE (circles)

d "X" (FAKE TRADITIONAL)

e (Chapter 2, #29)

f (Chapter 1, #3)

2 a (Chapter 1, #3) four times

b (Chapter 2, #28)

c (Chapter 2, #29) two times

d (Chapter 2, #42) moving Arm

A-B-A-C-G

3 a FIGURE 8 (Chapter 1 #8)

b FIGURE 8 REVERSE SIDEWAYS A-B-C
/FORWARD SPIN C-B-A (Chapter 2, # 47)

c FAKE (Chapter 1, #2)

d REVERSE A-B-C-B-A (Chapter 2, #21)

e Moving A-B-A-C / TOSS
(Chapter 2, #45)

4 a TOSS & PASS

b JUGGLE (Chapter 2, #58)

c SIMULTANEOUS (Chapter 2 #27-1)

d SWITCHING (Chapter 2, #11)

e FIGURE 8 (Chapter 1, #8)

f FIGURE 8 REVERSE SIDEWAYS A-B-C / FORWARD C-B-A (Chapter 2, #47)

5 a Do WALKING FORWARD A-B repeated, C one time (Chapter 2, #16)

b FAKE SPIN / TOSS (Chapter 2, #38)

c Roll OVER ALL FOUR FINGERS (Chapter 2, #70)

d Toss 1, 1½, 2, etc. (Chapter 2, #57)

e FAKE SPIN (Chapter 1, #2)

f Sideways A-B-C / REVERSE C-B-A (Chapter 2, #54)

g COUNTERCLOCKWISE A-B-C /
FORWARD SPIN C-B-A
Chapter 2, #52)

h COUNTERCLOCKWISE A-B /
FORWARD SPIN B-A,
(Chapter 2, #53)

i FORWARD SPIN G-A-B-A
(Chapter 2, #5)

j Fingertips (Chapter 2, #69)

k Exchange sticks (Chapter 1, #6)

6 a Thumb spin (Chapter 1, #5)

b Thumb spin COUNTER CLOCKWISE
(Chapter 2, #49)

c Thumb spin / ROLL OVER "O"
(Chapter 2, #50)

d Helicopter (if missed from above)
(Chapter 2, #9)

e Grip spin (Chapter 1, #1)

f Thumb spin FORWARD (Chapter 2, #51)

g TOSS FORWARD (Chapter 2, #60)

h TOSS (Chapter 1, #12)

i TOSS Snatch out of air (Chapter 2, #61)

7 a Toss CLOCKWISE / FORWARD FAKE (Chapter 2, #59)

b Figure 8, in A & B & C / FORWARD SPIN C-B-A (Chapter 2, #46)

c Figure 8 REVERSE SIDEWAYS A-B-C / FORWARD SPIN C-B-A (Chapter 2, #47)

d Improvise, using Chapter 2, #1 any pattern.

e Moving arm A-B-A-C / TOSS (Chapter 2, #45)

And last but certainly not least...

You can use your sticks to...

PLAY DRUMS

Drumstick Spinology™ Update

www.drstix.com

Keep sending in your thoughts, input, and new spins.

First of all, thank you all for your <u>relentless</u> enjoyment of Drumstick Spinology™ !! I have heard from a countless many of you and am always amazed at how many "spinning drummers" there are, and how enthusiastic we all are about our drumming and stick spinning.

For those of you who did not receive the DVD when we first published in October 2001, our apologies. If you purchased Drumstick Spinology™ up to December 2002 (either from SMG Publications or from anywhere else) and did not receive a DVD or VHS, please contact us with your address so that we can get it to you ASAP (upon verification of proof-of-purchase).

Dr.Stix ™

To continue to classify and develop Drumstick Spinology™ we have added two new chapters.

The first, Chapter 6, is for marching band and drum-line. Many of you have asked about the drum corps applications for Drumstick Spinology™ and have seen that once you get a good feel for the sticks...the sky is the limit. There are infinite choreographic possibilities in a drum-line or marching band, and here you will learn the basic "back sticking" moves and a few variations as well as "stick clicking".

The next, Chapter 7, is dedicated to health and the use of drumstick spinning for helping kids of all ages overcome learning disabilities, ADD/ADHD, and more. This was something totally unexpected, and it has been a joy working with Dr. Kuhn and seeing him help his patients using Drumstick Spinology™ !!!

Chapter 6 Drum line

Many of you have asked about Drumstick Spinology and how it can be applied to Marching Band, Drum Corps, and/or Drum-line. There are amazing adaptations using drumsticks and movement to create choreography for performance. The following are just a few of the basic ideas used for drum-line.

Back Sticking: This is a flashy way to add to your playing. It uses a back and forth motion.

For the right hand, hit the drum (Pic. A), then let the TIP come straight back so that you can hit with the END of the stick (Pic. B).

For the left hand (in Traditional grip) hit the drum (Pic. C) and then turn your wrist to the right bringing the END of the stick over to hit the drum with the END (Pic. D). You may want to raise your left elbow a bit.

Right hand Match grip R   Right hand Back Sticking Rb

Pic A   Pic B

Left hand Traditional L   Left hand Back Sticking Lb

Pic C   Pic D

Back Sticking exercises

Start working with the right hand by itself and hit R-Rb (see pictures A & B) back and forth several times until you get a smooth transition between the two. As always, practice slowly and get smooth. Once you are comfortable with that, do the same thing with your left hand L-Lb (see pictures C & D).
If you don't use Traditional grip, you can use Matched grip for the left hand. However, I find this a great way to "get a better grip" on Traditional grip. On the same note, you could try doing Traditional grip with both hands, this makes a great warm-up. Do not be in too much of a hurry. Once you get it going...it will fly!

The first application is to play two hits with your left hand in between each right hand hit.

Next play two hits with you right hand between each left hit. Notice that it starts with the right, and that the left plays back sticking first (Lb).

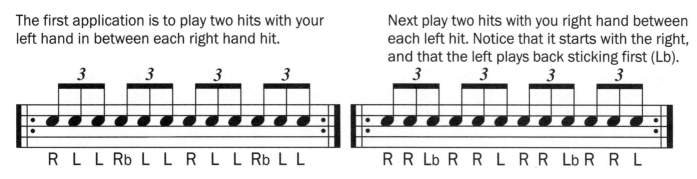

R L L Rb L L R L L Rb L L   R R Lb R R L R R Lb R R L

Developing this technique of two hits with the other hand will give you time to execute the back sticking.

Now put the two together:

R L L Rb L L R R Lb R R L

Once you get comfortable with these first basic patterns try to change the rhythm to this:

R L L Rb L L R R Lb R R L

Here is another one of my favorite applications. Great for your drum solos with a Latin feel.

R L L Rb L L R L R L L Rb L L R L

Now try this to switch sides (from starting with the right, to starting with the left):

R L L Rb L L R R L R R Lb R R L L

And finally, here is a great way to end any phrase that you are playing.

R L L Rb L R R Lb R R L

Stick Clicking:

I don't know if this if the official name for this technique, but I really like doing it, so that is what I have always called it. Although it may not be loud enough for all field applications, it certainly has its place in drumming.

NOTE: I also find this a great way to improve your Traditional grip.

Right stick strikes the top of the Left SHAFT. (Photo 1)
Right stick strikes (with the ANKLE) the bottom of the Left SHAFT. (Photo 2)
Left stick strikes the top of the Right stick with the Ankle (Photo 3)

Photo 1 TICK   Photo 2 TACK   Photo 3 TOCK

Notice that when you hit the TACK, not only does the right stick move up, but the left stick moves down to meet it. This will increase your speed immensely.

Try this pattern as steady quarter notes.

Next you will hit twice for the TICK sound (called TICK-Y). As always, start slow and get the right feel.

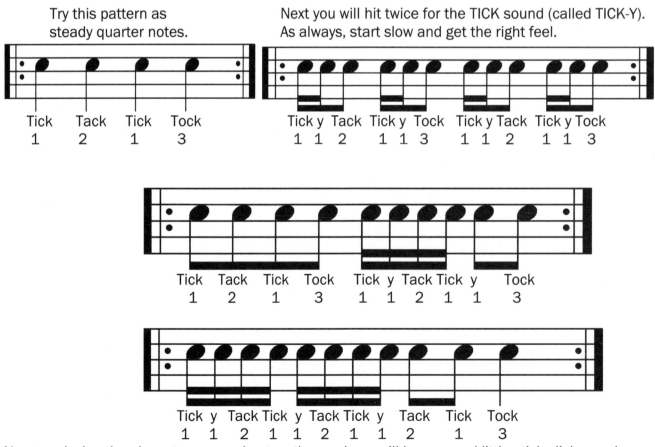

Tick   Tack   Tick   Tock
 1   2   1   3

Tick y Tack Tick y Tock Tick y Tack Tick y Tock
 1 1   2   1 1 3   1 1   2   1 1 3

Tick   Tack   Tick   Tock   Tick y Tack Tick y   Tock
 1   2   1   3   1   1   2   1   1   3

Tick y Tack Tick y Tack Tick y   Tack   Tick   Tock
 1   1   2   1   1   2   1   1   2   1   3

Now try playing the above two examples together and you will have a cool little stick click march.

76

HEALTHYSTIX ™

We are very proud and happy to announce that Drumstick Spinology is now being used in the healing world. Read on, and I hope that you are as inspired by what Dr. Kuhn has to say as I am.

"Healthystix" for Your Brain
by Kurt W. Kuhn, D.C., M.S.M., D.A.C.N.B.

It probably seems odd to see a section in a book on drumstick spinning written by a doctor who spends his days chasing down lesions in the brain. Imagine then how it was for Steve Stockmal who got an e-mail from me telling him how his book *Drumstick Spinology™,* was the best thing since sliced bread for kids with ADD/ADHD and other learning disorders.

For those of you who have an interest, I'll cover the science in just a moment. First I'd like to tell you about a little girl who was a patient of mine. She could light up a room with her smile. No kidding, it's a thousand watt smile. She came from a good home and even though her mother was a teacher, and even though she spent the time and worked hard, she had difficulty with math. She had never tested at her own grade level in math.

Her problem was on the opposite side of the brain compared to a young man who was also a patient of mine. He was diagnosed with attention deficit hyperactivity disorder (ADHD). He also was diagnosed with obsessive compulsive disorder and a few other things that can make it hard on an adolescent in high school.

While the symptoms were unique to each individual, the origin of the problem in both cases was the brain. The brain is like a muscle, you use it or you lose it. In both cases developmentally these kids skipped a step in their brain's development. Although it was not the same part of the brain affected, it happened for the same reason. It happened because the brain didn't get the input it needed from the environment to cause normal health, growth and development.

What's that got to do with *Drumstick Spinology™*? Simple. It was one of the therapies we used to rehabilitate these kids towards their potential. How well did it work? Excellent! For the first time that little girl tested at her grade level in math. And that young man will be listed in *Who's Who in American High School Students.* I believe they both can look forward to a whole new way of life.

Why does drumstick spinning work so well with these kids? The science aside, because the kids take the time do it because its fun! Of all the home care that I have prescribed, this is the one that gets done. You see, it's important to have these kids constantly increase the input to their nervous system in a way that exercises the weak neurological pathways. And after all, what kid doesn't want to be a rock star?

This is why you can look forward to more variations of spin material. Dr. Stix (alias Steve Stockmal) is working with me to give kids a chance to have a level playing field in school. That helps the kids and it also helps the drum community because for you drummers, that means chunked down information that is easy to digest on new and upcoming DVDs and books.

Drum rhythms and patterns are mapped in the brain. We'll be applying neurology to your drumming so that you strengthen your brain and improve your drum skills in the most neurologically efficient way. That translates into faster more accurate playing. I like what this does for the brain and drumming so much that I'm using it myself.

Credit must go to whom it is due. There are two people that are pioneers in this field and they are instrumental in the teaching of this information to the health professions. The leaders in applied neuroscience are Dr. Ted Carrick and Dr. Robert Melillo. They may be contacted via the Carrick Institute for Graduate Studies found in the contact information at the end of this section. I've also listed the information for how to contact the American Chiropractic Neurology Board (ACNB) in that same section if you are looking for a specialist in your area. The ACNB have a complete listing of board certified chiropractic neurologists world wide on their website. That should help you find a doctor close to you.

For you physicians and other science-heads, here's an over-simplification of an explanation for how it all works. Think of it as the *Reader's Digest* version of how stick spinning helps kids.

Every cell in the nervous system requires two things for its survival: fuel and activation. Fuel for the nervous system is oxygen and sugars. Activation is input from other nerves.

No fuel and the brain dies, we call that a stroke. No activation and the same thing can happen much slower, and we use less familiar terms like "transneural degeneration, retrograde chromatolysis or hypometabolism." These terms simply mean that when it comes to the nervous system, if you don't use it you lose it. In many ways the nervous system is like a muscle. If you don't use a muscle it becomes weaker and eventually will atrophy.

Nerves fire all or nothing just like MIDI. They are either "note on" or "note off," 1 or 0 after they become depolarized. Depolarization is the name for the chemical and electrical events that occur when a nerve fires. Depolarization happens either from "temporal or spatial summation."

"Temporal summation" is when enough individual impulses from a single source, which are individually too small to cause the nerve to fire, stack up on top of each other within a given time frame, and thus "summating" or adding up to become enough electrical charge to cause the nerve to hit it's threshold and fire. "Spatial summation" is when a nerve receives enough input from multiple different sources that create enough to add up, thus creating depolarization that causes the nerve to fire. These two methods (temporal and spatial summation) are what cause the nerve to fire to the muscles in your fingers when you spin a drumstick.

The nervous system sends messages to structures from 1 to 2 to 3... and so on. We doctors just use impressive names attached to the 1's, 2's and 3's (kind of like musicians who use fancy names to describe keys and scales). What matters is that all of these steps are necessary. If no 1, then no 2, or 3 and so on.

There is a pathway, really more of a chain that runs from your fingers to the very top of your brain. These are 12 longitudinal levels that we pass through along the way. When you spin a drumstick your hands, or rather the muscles of the fingers themselves, are the end organ in this chain of events (1). After your finger tips are receptors where the nervous system actually begins to recognize the spin (2). They bring input in from the muscles doing the drumstick spinning and pass them along to the nerves (3), which transfer the information into a nerve plexus (4). The information enters the posterior spinal root (5), then goes up the spinal cord (6), and passes up through the medulla (7), then the pons (8), cerebellum (9), mesencephalon (10), internal capsule (11) and finally up to the cortex (12) which is that wrinkly layer of gray matter of the brain. Easy, right?

So back in our chain of 1 to 2 to 3...12, 1 fires only when it gets enough input from its environment. The input can be anything that you can feel through your five senses (sight, sound, touch, smell and taste), gravity or even chemical events (food, medication, drugs, and even thoughts). In this case it is what you feel as you spin a drumstick that is the source of activation, that input which comes from the joint mechanoreceptors and the muscle spindles and causes the nerve to fire. Hang on; we are almost there!

If there is a problem with any of these longitudinal levels then the probability is that the brain will not get the activation it needs to survive at a healthy level. In other words, with less input coming in that will reduce the frequency of firing to the brain and that can cause it to function at a less than optimal way. Drumstick spinning in many patients can stimulate pathways in a way that can rehabilitate those structures.

You see, a loss of input to you drummers, means that you won't be playing anywhere near your rhythmical potential. But to a child whose system is operating at a deficit, that lack of input may mean they can't process information normally and will have a loss of executive function. By that I mean the ability to think and process normally.

The type of specialist who handles learning disorders and/or can evaluate your nervous system best for a drummer trying to optimize his playing is a chiropractic neurologist. A chiropractic neurologist is a specialist within the chiropractic profession who is especially skilled at observing for soft signs that are often the only way to diagnose these learning and behavioral conditions. They are also eminently qualified to help you drummers to achieve at your optimum neurological capability.

The chiropractic neurologist examines the individual and discovers any weakness in the nervous system. If any is found, then a plan is developed to rehabilitate the weak pathways and restore as much function as is possible in the individual. The results can be amazing. Kind of like the spins in this book.
Happy spinning! Kurt

Contact information:

For more information you may contact Dr. Kuhn at:

Kurt W. Kuhn, D.C., M.S.M., D.A.C.N.B.
1125 W. Fourth Street
Waterloo, IA 50702
USA
Telephone: 319-236-1000
Fax: 319-2347822
kurtkuhn@mchsi.com

For more information about chiropractic neurology and behavior or learning disorders contact:

Frederick R. Carrick, DC, PhD, D.A.C.N.B. or Robert J. Melillo D.C., D.A.B.C.N
Carrick Institute for Graduate Studies
203-8941 Lake Drive
Cape Canaveral, Florida
USA
Phone: 321-868-6464
Fax: 321-868-6468
www.carrickinstitute.org

For finding a chiropractic neurologist in your area contact the:

American Chiropractic Neurology Board
2803 Williams Drive, Suite 105
Georgetown, Texas 78628
USA
Telephone: (512) 863-2225
Fax (512) 863-2233
www.acnb.org

Other books by SMG Publications:

Drumstick Spinology - The complete method to spinning drumsticks   **$29.95**
                        (Includes 56-min instructional DVD)

The Music Teacher's Manual - Making Money Teaching Music   **$16.95**

DRUMology - Level 1   The beginner's drum set method   **$18.95**
                                 (Includes 1 play along CD)

DRUMology - Level 2   Intermediate drum set method   **$24.95**
                                 (Includes 2 play along CD's)

SMG PUBLICATIONS

Visit our website:

www.drstix.com

stevestockmal@yahoo.com